Poetic Contemplations

A Meditative Meandering through a World of Thoughts

Luke Mayo

BookLeaf Publishing

India | USA | UK

Dedication

This book is dedicated to all creative people, and all their audiences. Thank you for inspiring me and giving me a reason to do the poetry.

Preface

Those of us who have made an effort to live life will know that life is a mass of chaos, darkness, confusion and madness. Trying to deal with this, even briefly, can feel like a monumental struggle, and it's easy to question why we even bother.

Sometimes, we just need a little pick-me-up. We need a process, or method, to help us through the struggles we face. We need a form of emotional release, to assuage the torments we feel on a regular basis.

The poetry you'll find in this book is the result of my emotional release. Writing this poetry has given me a purpose and a motivation to face the struggles of my life. You are welcome to read it, and I hope it means something to you. Perhaps it might inspire you to find your own methods for dealing with your struggles.

If I can do it, so can you. You just need to find a way that works for you.

Acknowledgements

My life has a number of notable contributors, of which I am just one. I pay tribute to some of those good people here and now.

University of Suffolk, BookLeaf Publishing, Pop My Mind and the Global Panorama are just some of the people who have empowered me, encouraged me and indulged me in my creative pursuits. My voice and passion is owed to them, and I will always be grateful.

My main career has been based in the charity and public sectors, and the jobs I've had therein include, without being limited to, Open Road Visions, Essex Police, Essex Libraries and Broomfield Hospital. All of these workplaces, and many more, have inspired a great deal of my poetic ideas, and for that I thank them hugely.

Lastly, and mostly, my family. Without them, my life would not be a tiny fraction of what it currently is. Their support and presence has enabled me to do the good things I've done. I love them a great deal.

Ta muchly.

1. Legends of the Periphery

Have you ever had that feeling?

Where unseen eyes watch you?
Where shadows dance in the corner of your sight
Where the breeze whispers silent messages?

I think there are people there
Souls unknown to us
Living their lives in another dimension
Those moments when we feel their presence
That's the gateway between worlds

Who are these people?
Maybe they're like us
They could be heroes
Legends in their own right

Perhaps we'll meet one day
Who knows what the future holds?

2. To Dream or To Do?

The human soul is made of dreams
The world is made of actions
Life happens when the soul meets the world

It's good to dream
It's great to make dreams real
Better a small dream you can do
Than a big dream too big for doing

Live for the small dream
The tiny ambitions dotting the path ahead
Scattering our future like flowers to collect
Trophies behind us when we achieve them

No dream is too small to be worth doing
Every dream deserves fulfilment

Tell me your dreams with the excitement of lovers
I will listen with awe and wonder
For dreams give us a reason to live

3. Voices of the Past

Every word hurled against me
Weaponised to wound me
I remember them all
Swirling in my mind endlessly
Like stones in a whirlpool
Taunting me as they draw into view

Dragging me down
Holding me back
Never letting me go
A selfish cycle of hate

It's a good thing I have my own voice

It counters hate with love
It reminds me that I am worthy
It assures me that I am better than my taunts

Say what you want about me
My voice speaks too
Calmly guiding me through the onslaught of insults
Supplying wisdom to help me with the darkness

We all have a kind inner voice
We'd do well to pay heed

4. Primal Mysteries

Why does wet paint scream to be touched?
Why do I stand at the edge and imagine the jump?
Why do I indulge the darkness immediately before bed?
Why do I lock my gaze at car crashes?

Time and again
An endless loop
My mind returns to what terrifies it
Circling the scene like a predator on prey
Seeking the gates of hell and making a home there

I don't know what freedom feels like
It might be worse than captivity
That's why freedom is itself captivating
Drawn to the marvel of fearful feelings
Resistance is irresistible

It doesn't make sense
Yet I think of it still
For thinking is endless
An escape with no escape

5. Failed by Who I Am

I'm so sorry
What else can I say?
Turns out I'm not what you're looking for

I tried to be the one for you
Your needs were mine to meet
I slayed demons to reach your standards
Your approval was my Holy Grail

Also like the Holy Grail
Your approval was not mine to have
My highest was too low for you
My best did nothing for you
I failed you just by being me

I'll never know what you wanted
I just know it wasn't me
I might be good
But not good for you
That snuffs out the light in me

You will always be my impossible dream
My forbidden fruit

The worst thing is
I'll be nothing to you

6. Haunted by Dread

Taunting behind my back
Laughing in my face
Screaming in my head
That's where Dread is found

In empty rooms it tricks me with watching eyes
On crowded streets it tells me all souls judge me
During hours of sleep it parades my failures before me

Everywhere I go it joins me
Stalks me
Mocks me
My lifelong companion
The cruel master that is Dread
Ensnaring and bombarding me

Every person is its tool
Every interaction is its trap
Weaponised against me in humiliation

Nowhere is safe
Nothing is sacred
No time is time off

Welcome to my existence
Locked in a Dreadful dance

7. Waking Dreams and Perma-Nightmares

Every time I close my eyes they come
When I open my eyes they are with me still
The demons of my life
Rendering me sleepless and wakeless

In the corner of my eye
At the back of my mind
They watch me from the shadows
They follow me wherever I go
Sleep is no escape from them
For they make dreams as real as reality

I can explain my demons to nobody
For the demons ensnare and distort my words
They make me and themselves misunderstood
They remove me from my friends
Standing in their place
Grinning obscenely at their power

But they fail to notice
I have power too
I can't stop the nightmare
But I can take the reins

They invade my space
But the space is still mine

The demons want a nightmare
I'll give them one

8. Mask Becomes Me

You know in health emergencies
The way people have to wear masks?
Nobody seems to realise
I'm already wearing one

I've worn it all my life
For protection
For safety
For necessity

Nobody likes who I am
So I hide who I am behind a mask
Now nobody knows who I am
Not even me any more

Sometimes I wonder
What happens when the mask falls?
 Will a demon emerge?
 Will I cease to exist?
The mask is all I know
Removing the mask removes me

I'm not scared of what takes the mask's place
I'm scared that nothing ever will

9. The Monsters Among Us

They say that monsters are good hiders
This I know for I've seen their masks
The worst thing is they're my friends' faces

The scariest thing is not when they get you
The scariest thing is when they trick you first
Trust is earned before it is broken
The earning makes the pain of breaking more exquisite
This is exactly what the monsters crave

Viciousness is the blood soaring through their veins
Despair is their source of sustenance to gorge
Fakery is their mode of transport

They even fake being indestructible
But I've seen their weak spot

Ignore them and watch them starve

The slaying monsters is the sweet part
Watching false friends die is the bitter part

10. Intrusion of Anxious Thoughts

Like unruly kids in a classroom lesson
Like gobby businessmen in a meeting suite
Desperate for attention and never letting up

These are the anxious thoughts of my mind

An endless chatter of tension is what they supply
Sometimes ignorable
Sometimes consuming
Always present

They call the shots
They smirk at their power
At least they once did
For I have found my own power

They retain their residence in me
But like wild hounds on leashes
They don't walk me
I walk them

When anxious thoughts intrude
I assert myself

11. The Making of Heroes

What are stars?
Lights that burn bright in deepest darkness
What are blades?
Metal battered and forged in fire
What are heroes?
Ordinary people who don't quit in extraordinary
difficulty

Every path before us is laden with struggles
Mountains to climb
Furnaces to survive
Darkness to navigate

 Do we crash and burn?
Do we push ahead?
Do we hide away?
Do we find our strength?
Do we fade to nothing?
Do we survive and thrive?

With a good cause to guide us
And loyal friends beside us
The choice is always ours

If you need a hero
Look within yourself
When life gets dark
The inner hero brings the light

12. The Shiftings of Consciousness

When people speak of moments
I never know what they mean
How do you measure a moment?
 When does a moment end and the next begin?
Is a moment the same for you as it is for me?
From one moment to another
Will we be closer together?
 Or will we be further away?

What about friendship?
Opinions vary beyond recognition
There are many people I consider friends
Do they think of me as a friend?
Do they think of me at all?
My lifelong dream is a place in peoples' hearts
Am I chasing an illusion?

We're told to make our dreams a reality
But we're never told which is which
Reality is abstract
Abstract is changeable
Change is all that's left
Do dreams stop being dreams when they become real?

Is reality unreal if it was dreamed first?

I don't know what reality is
Maybe I'll never know
Maybe reality is unknowable
Maybe that's ok

13. When Martyrdom Fails

I have a passion for good deeds
In a world where passion and good deeds are not
accepted
They are rejected
They are derided
They are abandoned

What am I supposed to do?
When all I have to offer is wanted by nobody?
When the things people want repulse me?
When a world screaming for conformity is my
anathema?

I want to give myself to a cause
But there are none available
Nothing on the shelves but vapidity and vacuousness
The only goal of recognized worth is instant gratification
Sacrifice is ignored for new demands and desires

The world and I have nothing in common
People need a hero and I want to be one
But we can't agree on what heroism is
The world wants a hero it can use and toss aside
But this is not who I am

I no longer what to save the world
I need to escape it

14. Embrace the Ordinary

Look at what happens in our world
Quirks are worshipped
Normal is boring
Boring is demonized

Intolerance of difference is intolerable
Also intolerable are sameness, routine and regularity
Difference once shunned is now promoted for
celebration
Normality is outlawed and sealed off for oblivion

Some of us gravitate to the reassurance of routine
We need this to survive
But the rebels take it from us
They make us pariahs for being ourselves
We yearn for peace alongside the quirky ones
But instead they shame and shun us

They say we're slaves
They say we're drones
They say we're captives

We know who we are
We're not the underdog

We work to keep society afloat
We do what needs to be done

We don't care about doing something different
We care about doing something good
This is the duty of embracing the ordinary

15. Saving the Saviours

The world loves its everyday heroes
Defenders of life, love, law, and liberty
It grandstands them
But does it care for them?
Who serves as the heroes' heroes?

They risk it all
They take it on
No deed undone
No sacrifice unmade
Then when it's over
They lie broken
Who is there for them?
Who honours their story?

The price of heroism
Words of praise but no deeds of respect
Salvation of others through them
None left over for themselves

When I am delivered from torment
Questions hang over me?
Who paid the price?
Who is left with the fallout?

Anonymous they may be
They still receive my silent thanks

It's the least I can do

16. Filling of the Glasses

Is your glass half-empty or half-full?
My glass is never full
For my glass is limitless in its opportunities

I am a veritable cocktail of emotions
Vibrant joy mixed in with festering sorrow
Dashes of simmering rage thrown in for measure
A cluster of neuroses shaken and stirred

My emotions are boundless and unified
Not a single one displaces another
All engage and interact at full strength
Laughs and sobs perpetually echo through my neural
paths

My sadness may expand in potency
Taking anxiety in rise along with it
They will never sap my joy
Nor crush my peace
Nor diminish my hope

My feelings submit to me
They strengthen and enrich me

That's why I sup from the glasses of emotion
They are my elixir of life

17. Harmony of Broken Spirits

The monsters who break people
They all have something in common
They once were broken too

Those of us whom the monsters break
We also can choose to become monsters
Or we can choose to help and heal each other

What will you choose to do?

The monsters catch up with us all eventually
They herald a damage we cannot escape
What we do with the damage is up to us

Do we hide away in the wreckage?
Do we pass the pain to other like a disease?
Do we call the monstrous cycle to a halt?
Do we replace that cycle with a better one?

The choice is ours
And the choice may change
If you regret your choice
Feel free to change your mind

18. A Glitch in Time

A lifetime of material in my neural paths
It's a shame that the footage has parts missing

Taking a stroll down my lane of memories
Why are there so many scenes I fail to recognize?
 Why are the scenes I do recognize not here?
Has someone been stealing my past experiences?
I wouldn't know since I can't remember

Where I once had warm youthful nostalgia
All I hold now is sterile emptiness
Friendly voices used to resound through my ear
The echo of white noise is all that remains today

When did my memories fade to non-existence?
 Did they exist to begin with?
What does this day for my relationship skills?
 Even my past abandons me

Wary unease is my only companion now
I don't care for it much

19. A Relationship of Alternate Realities

Do you really love me?
Or do you love the ego boost I give you?
Do I really love you?
Or do I love the purpose I feel being with you?
Are you scared to lose me?
Or are you scared to lose the validation I bring you?
 Am I scared to lose you?
 Or am I scared to lose the only person who tolerates
me?

A relationship of this or that
One interpretation or another
Like a mirror reflection
But the reflection is demented
We never speak of the underside which stalks us
The subtle subtext which sleeps in shadows
It's the dimension of nowhere
The place where relationships doss down and die

Relationships like ours
Combining a pristine surface with a hollow base
There is violence in silence
Will we be its latest casualty?

Maybe we should talk it out

20. Shadow of the Moon

Do you ever think of the moon?
Sometimes I do

I find myself in a contemplation
I consider the moon's other side
The side hidden from view
The dark and lonely places
Untouched by the sun
Unseen by people
Unknown by everyone

The moon and I are two of a kind
We share much in common
We both are only partly seen and half unknowable
Some of our ways are drenched in shadows

I don't know if people really see me
Their eyes might be tinted by false ideas of me
Romanticised and demonized by factors beyond me
Storied told behind my back with no word of truth

Do you think the moon vibes with me?
Probably as much as a flying space rock can
It just carries on and does its thing

Maybe I should do the same
If the moon can be a symbol of stoicism
Perhaps I can too

21. Distortions of Perceptions

My favourite places are tranquil surroundings
I hope one day they'll help pacify the turmoil within me
It's a shame that my pursuits of calmness come to nothing
For any and all attempts are scuppered by my ravaged mind

The popular notion is that reading soothes the soul
I would love to agree with this assertion
But for my brain's warped disruptions of words
Sentence structures rearrange and derail before my eyes
I wonder if my eyes are responsible for it

Characters interchange each other's identities
Then their identities disintegrate
Only I remain as reader
At least for now

Even music struggles to penetrate my cerebral barriers
Lyrical waxes decay into dissonant screeches
Notes and chords alike twisted and set to tumble
I'm sad for the creative souls who birthed these tunes
They weren't expecting their creations to be mangled

For that's what my mind's filters do

What music could be made of my spirit's incoherence?
Would anyone dare to listen?
Perhaps they'd make more sense of it than me